Socially Connected

A social distancing manifesto

Compiled by Leslie Osornio

THIS BOOK IS A COMMUNITY EFFORT

Socially
Connected

It began as a desperate call for motivation on Instagram, and developed into a therapeutic support system for everyone who is collectively losing their mind alone.

We are undergoing an unprecedented situation. As a species, we are defined by our socializing abilities and our communities. As such, distancing is a difficult mission. Remember, there is not a right way to do something that's never been done before.

Whether our community consists of those living in our household, or the Online community we have curated, we are not alone. Now more than ever we are connected, we are valid, and we will endure.

1

Mental health first!

smoke some pot

2

KE
your friends & family
CL

EP

OSE

The ones you live with.

NOT the other ones.

3

Get as much **sun** as possible

This is a solitary act

4

Escape your current reality

with *friends...*

5

R

RE

EA

EA

AD

yes, books are still a thing

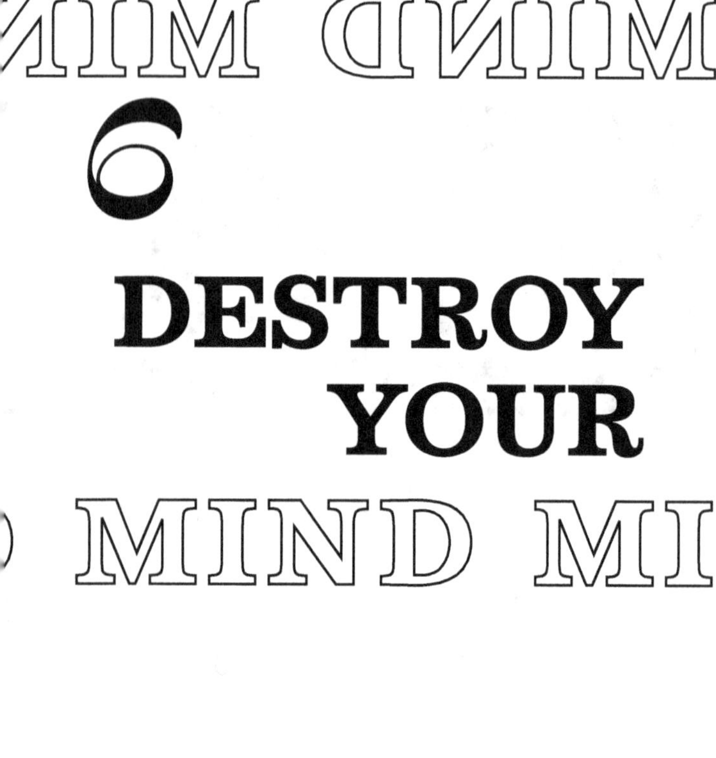
6
DESTROY
YOUR
MIND

ONE VIDEO GAME AT A TIME.

7

Explore

Unorthodox

methods of *communication.*

8

CRY WHEN NECESSARY

9

eep a constant stream
usic, TV, Audible, dog
r hear your own thoug
f noise at all time. Mus
he goal is to never hea
onstant stream of nois
le, dog whistles. The go
oughts. **Keep a consta**
time. Music, TV, Audib
is to never hear your o
tream of noise at all ti
histles. The goal is to n
eep a constant stream
udible, dog whistles. Th
wn thoughts. Keep a co
me. Music, TV, Audible

noise at all time.

istles. The goal is to ne

. Keep a constant strea

TV, Audible, dog whist

our own thoughts. Kee

t all time. Music, TV, A

is to never hear your

stream of noise at all

dog whistles. The goal

thoughts. Keep a cons

. Music, TV, Audible, d

ver hear your own thou

noise at all time. Musi

goal is to never hear y

tant stream of noise a

og whistles. The goal i

10

work on your relationships. Especially with

your
self

You need it.

11

CyBeR

HIIT circuits

ReCrEa

yoga in your bedroom with strangers.

ACTi

indoor cycling

30 sec abs commercial breaks

GrOUp

virtual hikes

TIoNal

running in place

iTiEs

water jugs as weights

It's everything you've **never** wanted to experience.

12

Remember when you said...

“I just wish I could spend more time with my pet(s)”

well.

13

irrit

Relish **the fact that you don't have to see**

rrita

ting

the irritating people you normally deal with.

ting

14

15

PRESERVE YOUR SANITY.

SANITY.
SANITY.
SANITY.
SANITY.
SANITY.
SANITY.

SANITY.
SANITY.
SANITY.
SANITY.
SANITY.
SANITY.
SANITY.
SANITY.
SANITY.

scream occasionally

16

PLAN FOR THE FUTURE

This *will* **end at some point.**

17

SO ROOM ACTI

MUCH

FOR

ITIES

18

Further your knowledge of **polytheistic beliefs...**

Astrology.

(welcome to the age of Aquarius)

19

It's all about BALANCE.

NCE.BALA
BALANCE.
NCE.BALA
BALANCE.
NCE.BALA
BALANCE.
NCE.BALA
BALANCE.

Watch six hours of *Tiger King*, followed by six hours of anything that will better your life IN ANY WAY AT ALL.

20

Wor

kout

Now we know why people in jail are so buff.

21

THOSE THOUGHTS YOU'D NEVER SHARE?

Write them down.
#AnneFrankVibes

22

Most Importantly:

Most Importantly:

Most Importantly:

Most Importantly:

Most Importantly:

Most Importantly:

Most Importantly:

Most Importantly:

Most Importantly:

Most Importantly:

Most Importantly:

Show gratitude whenever possible

COLOPHON

This book was made with one typeface. Al-bight a widely varied typeface. Temeraire, in regular, bold, and italienne italic.

The advice, that should only be followed loosely, was provided by a collective group of instagram users. Namely, Peter, Darryl, Devon, Macy, George, Ameligh, Fernanda, Hope, Dallas, Tucker, Tafari, Nicco, Imitzy, Manny, Tyra, and Shelby. Thank you for your inspiring words.

This book was printed and published through lulu, an on demand print house and is made just for you. Yes you. Happy Quarantine.

Socially
Connected

www.ingramcontent.com/pod-product-compliance
Lightning Source LLC
Chambersburg PA
CBHW061737250726
48657CB00002B/977

* 9 7 8 1 7 1 6 9 4 1 9 3 1 *